SEARCH-AND-FIND
A NUMBER OF NUMBERS

A Chapter Two book
created by Amanda Wood and Mike Jolley

Brimming with creative inspiration, how-to projects, and useful information to enrich your everyday life, Quarto Knows is a favourite destination for those pursuing their interests and passions. Visit our site and dig deeper with our books into your area of interest: Quarto Creates, Quarto Cooks, Quarto Homes, Quarto Lives, Quarto Drives, Quarto Explores, Quarto Gifts, or Quarto Kids.

A Number of Numbers © 2020 Quarto Publishing plc.
Text © 2020 Amanda Wood and Mike Jolley
Illustrations © 2020 Allan Sanders

First published in 2019 by Wide Eyed Editions, an imprint of The Quarto Group.
400 First Avenue North, Suite 400, Minneapolis, MN 55401, USA.
T (612) 344-8100 F (612) 344-8692 **www.QuartoKnows.com**

A catalogue record for this book is available from the British Library.

ISBN 978-1-78603-537-0

The illustrations were created digitally.
Set in HVD Bodedo

Published by Rachel Williams
Designed by Tracey Cunnell
Edited by Amanda Wood
Production by Dawn Cameron

Manufactured in Shenzhen, China PP112019

9 8 7 6 5 4 3 2 1

SEARCH-AND-FIND
A NUMBER OF NUMBERS

Allan Sanders

WIDE EYED EDITIONS

Welcome to A Number of Numbers!

Over the following pages you'll find lots of things to count, from animals on an ark to objects in the ocean, snowballs in a ski resort to instruments in the orchestra. At first there's just a few things for you to find in each picture—so use your fingers to help keep track and you'll soon get the hang of it, and by the end of the book you'll be counting all the way to **100!**

In some pictures there's more than one set of things to find so you're going to be pretty busy. And there might be some other puzzles for you to solve along the way too—like matching pairs or finding other things hidden in the pictures—so keep your eyes peeled (which means look really carefully at each scene).

If you're looking for lots of things it's sometimes a good idea to start by looking at the top left hand corner of each scene and work your way across and then down each page so you don't miss anything. It might help to keep a pencil and paper handy too so you can make a note of how many things you've found as you go.

So, good luck, flex those fingers, and start counting!

SEARCH-AND-FIND
A NUMBER OF NUMBERS

Allan Sanders

WIDE EYED EDITIONS

Welcome to A Number of Numbers!

Over the following pages you'll find lots of things to count, from animals on an ark to objects in the ocean, snowballs in a ski resort to instruments in the orchestra. At first there's just a few things for you to find in each picture—so use your fingers to help keep track and you'll soon get the hang of it, and by the end of the book you'll be counting all the way to **100!**

In some pictures there's more than one set of things to find so you're going to be pretty busy. And there might be some other puzzles for you to solve along the way too—like matching pairs or finding other things hidden in the pictures—so keep your eyes peeled (which means look really carefully at each scene).

If you're looking for lots of things it's sometimes a good idea to start by looking at the top left hand corner of each scene and work your way across and then down each page so you don't miss anything. It might help to keep a pencil and paper handy too so you can make a note of how many things you've found as you go.

So, good luck, flex those fingers, and start counting!

1
ONE

Our number fun has just begun so let us start with number **1**!

Can you find ten things that only appear once in this picture?

1 wheel, **1** hot air balloon, **1** flower, **1** watch, **1** hat, **1** parrot, **1** butterfly, **1** mustache, **1** monocle, and **1** bow tie.

What other **1**s can you find?

2
TWO

The animals went in 2 by 2...

There are 20 pairs of animals on the ark. Can you count them all?

Look carefully because some of them might be trying to hide!

What else can you find 2 of in the picture?

seagull

gorilla

frog

rhino

elephant

tiger

leopard

dolphin

zebra

3

THREE

Fairytales and nursery rhymes are often full of **3**s.

Here are **3** blind mice. Which one's got the cheese?

Here are **3** bears having their breakfast, but where's Goldilocks?

Here are **3** billy-goats gruff, trip-trotting across the bridge, but where's the troll?

Now can you find **3** little pigs, **3** houses, **3** swans, **3** butterflies, **3** toadstools, **3** letters, **3** pigeons, **3** flowers, **3** trees, **3** snails, and **1** big, bad wolf?

4
FOUR

How many seasons in a year?
Yes, you're right. It's **4**!

SPRING

Can you count **1** rabbit, **2** bees,
3 Easter eggs, and **4** skippy lambs?

What else can you see?

SUMMER

Can you count **1** ice cream, **2** starfish,
3 spades, and **4** sandcastles?

What else can you see?

FALL

Can you count **1** witch, **2** squirrels,
3 acorns, and **4** pumpkins?

What else can you see?

WINTER

Can you count **1** sled, **2** Christmas puddings,
3 robins, and **4** snowballs?

What else can you see?

5
FIVE

Counting to **5** is simply grand—
Just use the fingers on your hand!

Can you find these things embroidered on the woolly glove?

 **1 reindeer**

 2 penguins

 **3 snowmen**

 4 snowflakes

 **5 fir trees**

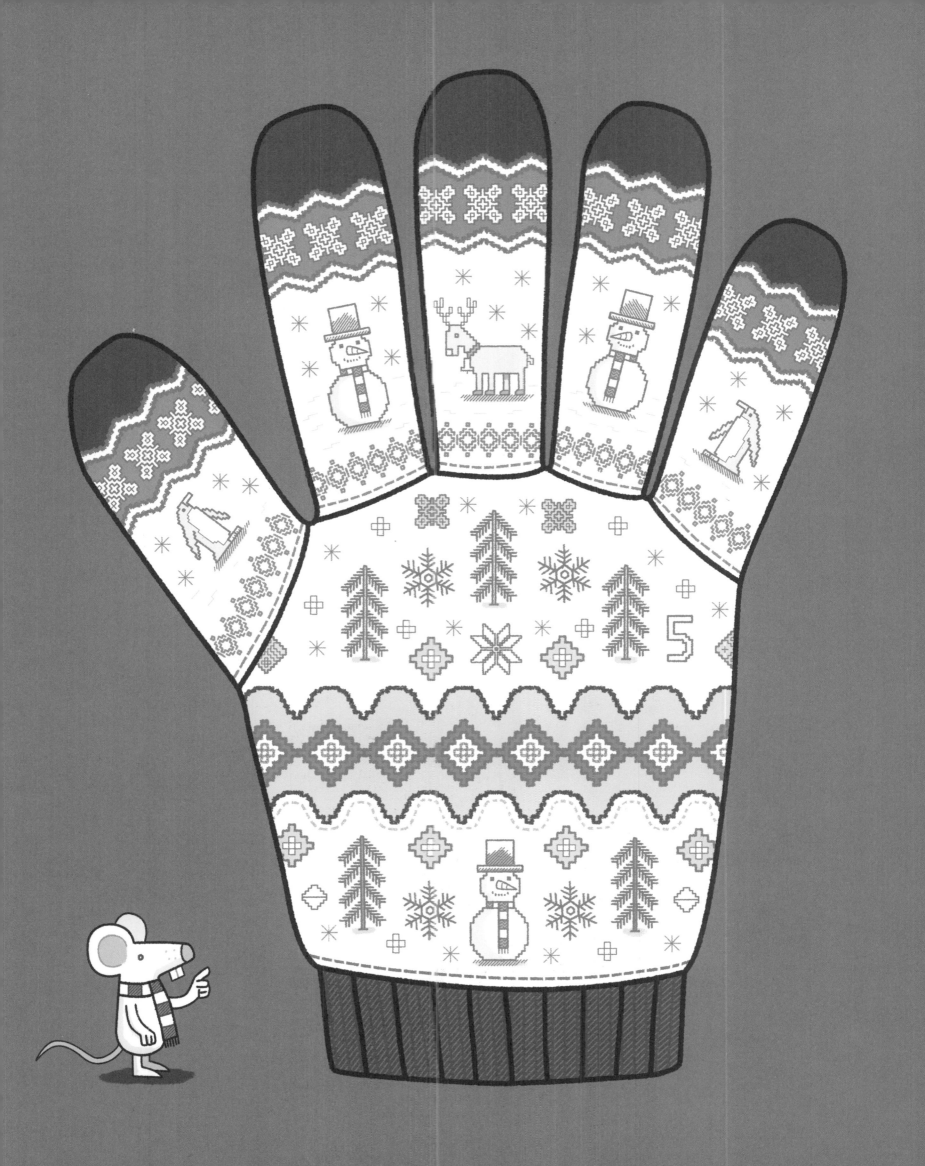

6 SIX

dragon

castle

king

YE OLDE FORGE.

shield

horse

musician

ox

cannon

The king is in his castle,
but what else can you see?

Can you find
6 cannonballs,
6 brave knights,
6 treasure chests,
6 flags, **6** shields,
and **6** golden keys.

flag

golden key

VI

eagle

sword

queen

knight

cannonball

portcullis

treasure chest

NO JUNK MAIL

wizard

drawbridge

moat

7

SEVEN

Can you find 7 different dogs and their matching pups?

Now look for 7 balls, 7 bowls, 7 bones, and 1 tasty hot dog!

BEST IN SHOW

1ST

ROSIE

MILO

MAX

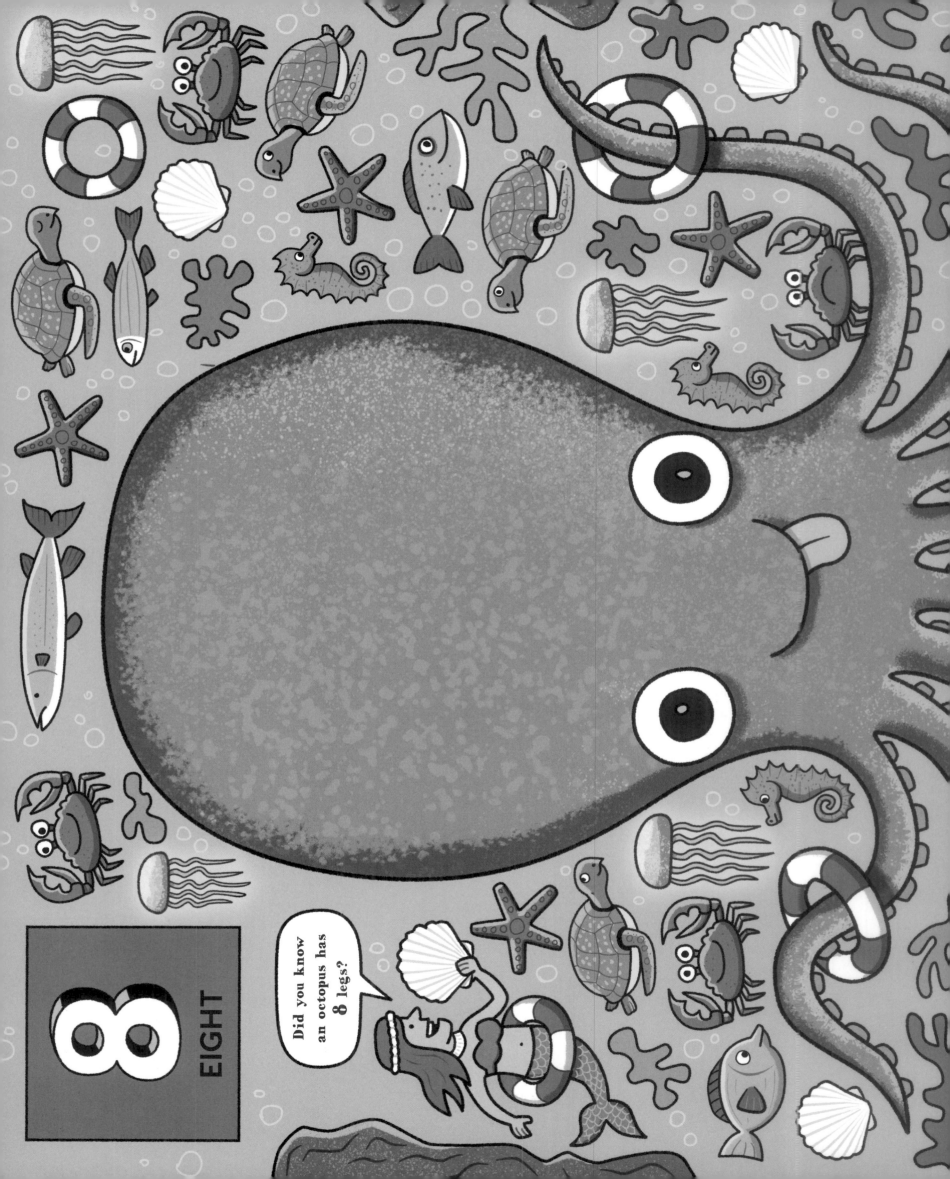

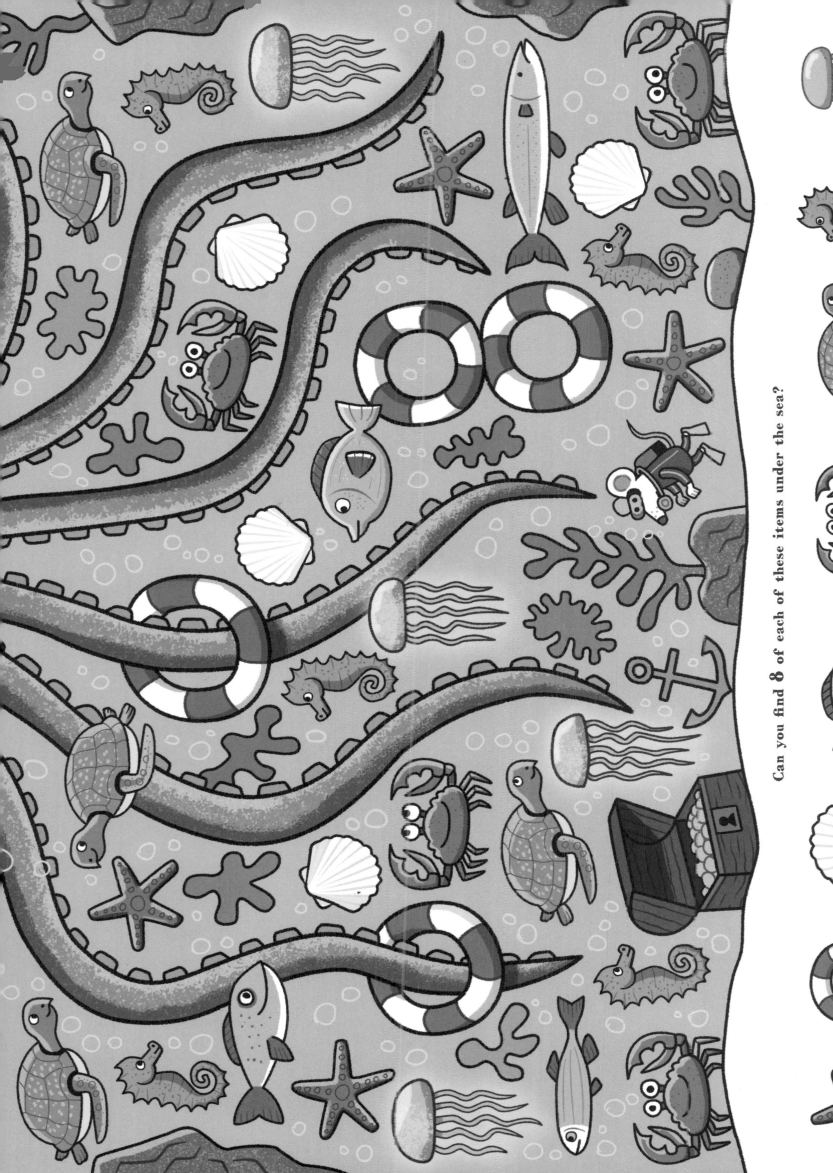

Can you find 8 of each of these items under the sea?

 jellyfish

 seahorse

 turtle

 crab

 fish

shell

lifebelt

starfish

Can you find **9** odd socks, **9** jumpers, **9** missing shoes, **9** t-shirts, **9** pairs of glasses, **9** gloves, **9** pairs of underpants, **9** hats, and **9** pairs of trousers?

What other clothes can you see?

10
TEN

Can you find all of these yummy items at the picnic?

1 jell-o

2 pies

3 jars of jelly

4 ice creams

5 cookies

Can you find **10** buzzing bees?

6 apples

7 sandwiches

8 cups of coffee

9 glasses of juice

10 cupcakes

11
ELEVEN

All aboard the Mystery Express, but who's on board the train today?

Can you find these **11** passengers --a chef, a clown, a king, a nun, a judge, a nurse, a fireman, a fisherman, a shepherd, a photographer, and a basketball player?

Now look harder and see if you can spot **11** detectives and
one naughty bank robber, but where has he hidden his loot?

Can you find **12** pigeons and their lost eggs in this busy city scene?

Now see if you can spot these **12** things in the picture—a cyclist, a crane, a skateboard, a cat, a fruit bowl, a jogger, a gnome, a weight-lifter, a bird cage, a robot, and Superman!

How many of these **13** creepy things can you find?

black cats
witches
ghosts
skulls
frogs
spiders
snails
crows
gravestones
pumpkins
bones
broomsticks
werewolves

helicopter

chalet

fir tree

snowboarder

skier

snowmobile

NORTH POLE

igloo

15
FIFTEEN

Let's count up to **15** on the farm.

Can you find:

1 scarecrow

2 cats

3 horses

4 pigs

5 gates

6 cows

7 sheep

8 ducks

9 turnips

10 logs

11 chickens
(and one cockerel)

12 carrots

13 crows

14 rain boots

15 apples

CARROTS

17 SEVENTEEN

Who's lost in the maze?

Can you match **17** lost items with their correct owners?

18

EIGHTEEN

It's crazy golf time! Can you find **18** golf balls and **18** flags in the picture?

Who else can you see whom you've met before in this book?

19
NINETEEN

Oh dear! The forgetful
scientist has left all sorts
of things inside the robot.

Take a look and see if
you can find them all.

What else can you see?

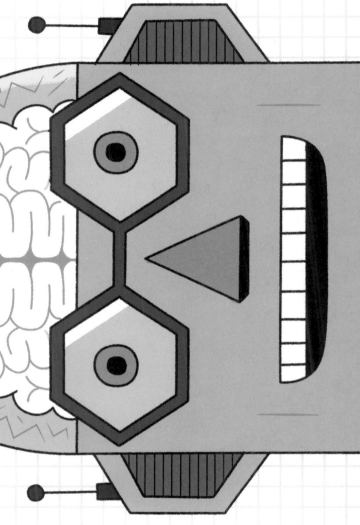

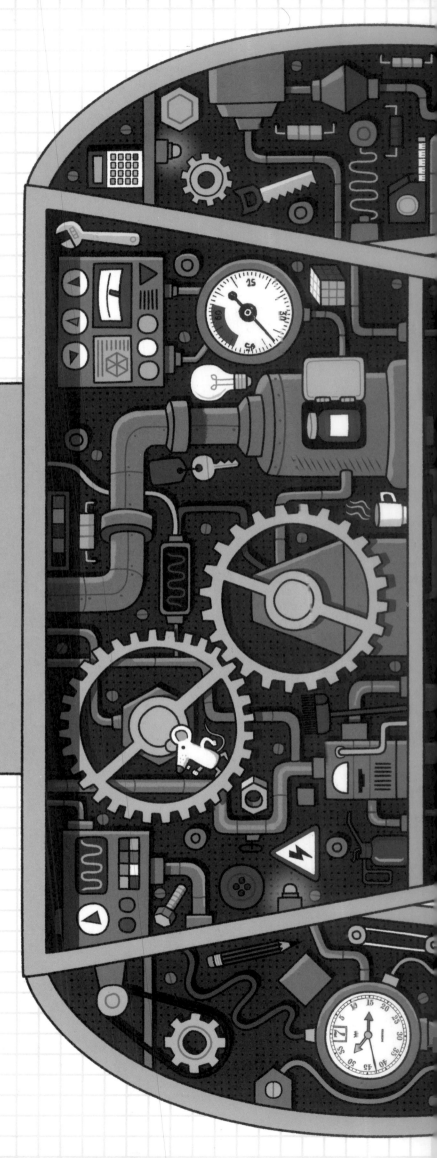

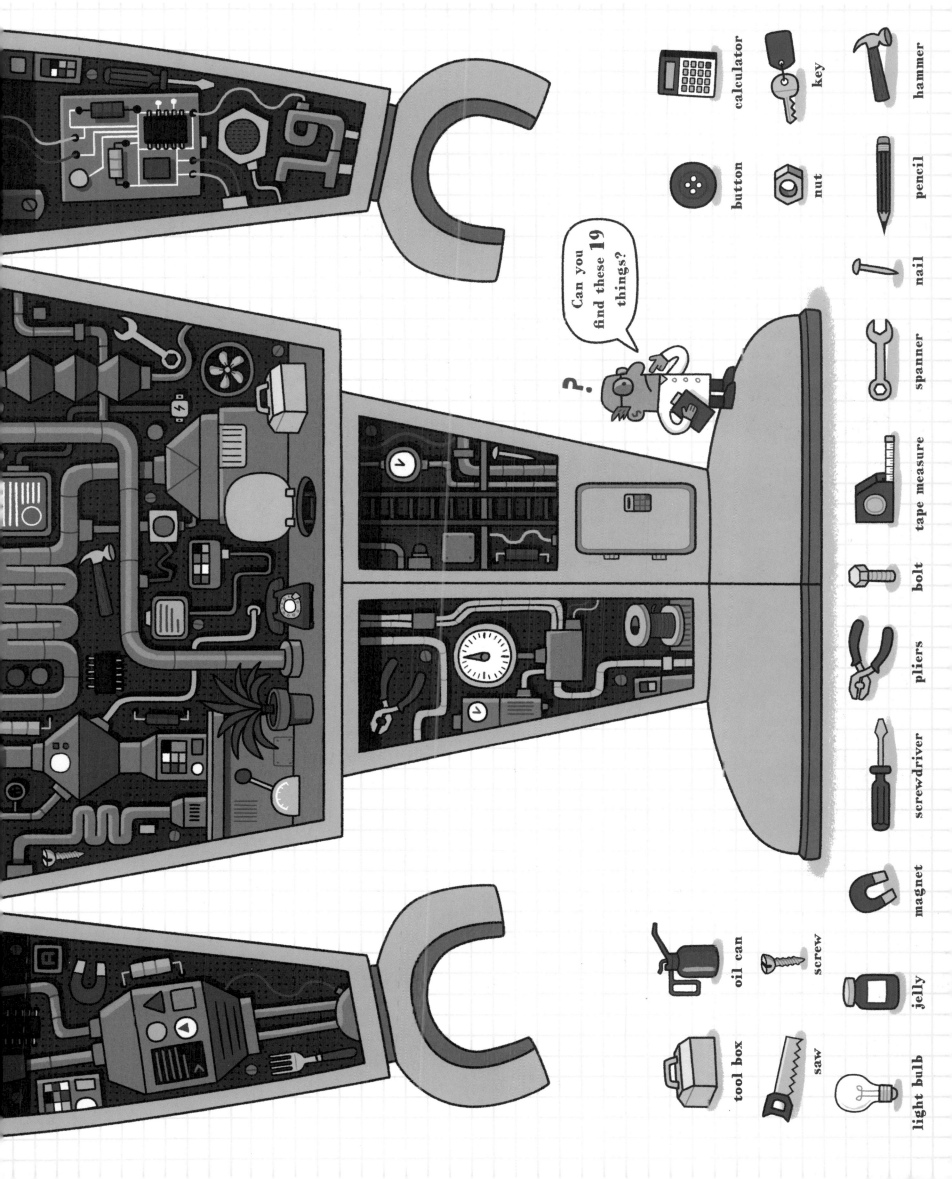

There are lots of instruments in the concert hall. See if you can find them all!

20
TWENTY

Let's count up to **20** by finding all these things in the orchestra.

1 triangle

2 pianos

3 tubas

4 xylophones

5 harps

6 cellos

7 trombones

8 french horns

9 trumpets

10 hand bells

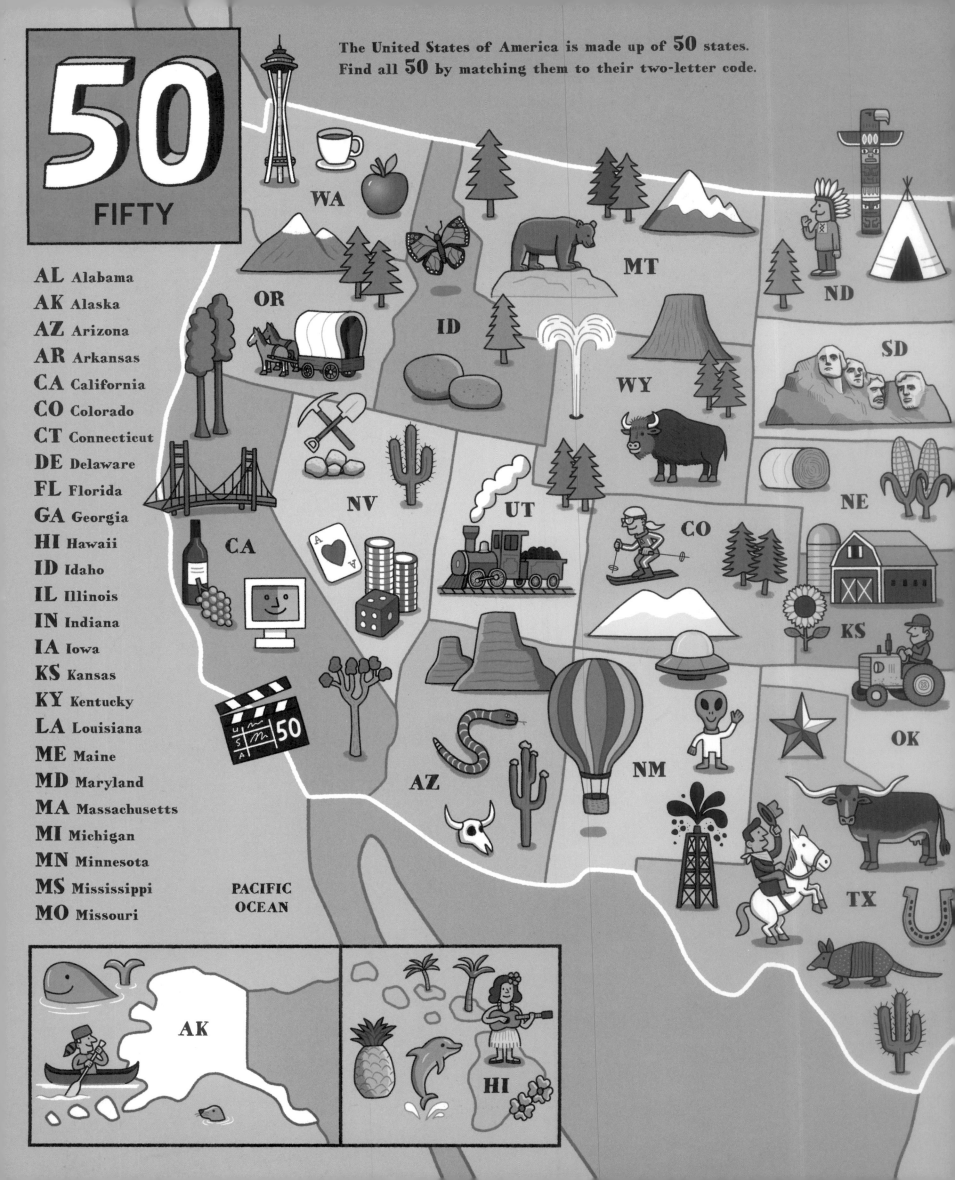

50
FIFTY

The United States of America is made up of **50** states. Find all **50** by matching them to their two-letter code.

AL Alabama
AK Alaska
AZ Arizona
AR Arkansas
CA California
CO Colorado
CT Connecticut
DE Delaware
FL Florida
GA Georgia
HI Hawaii
ID Idaho
IL Illinois
IN Indiana
IA Iowa
KS Kansas
KY Kentucky
LA Louisiana
ME Maine
MD Maryland
MA Massachusetts
MI Michigan
MN Minnesota
MS Mississippi
MO Missouri

WA
OR
ID
MT
ND
SD
WY
NV
UT
CO
NE
KS
CA
AZ
NM
OK
TX

PACIFIC
OCEAN

AK

HI

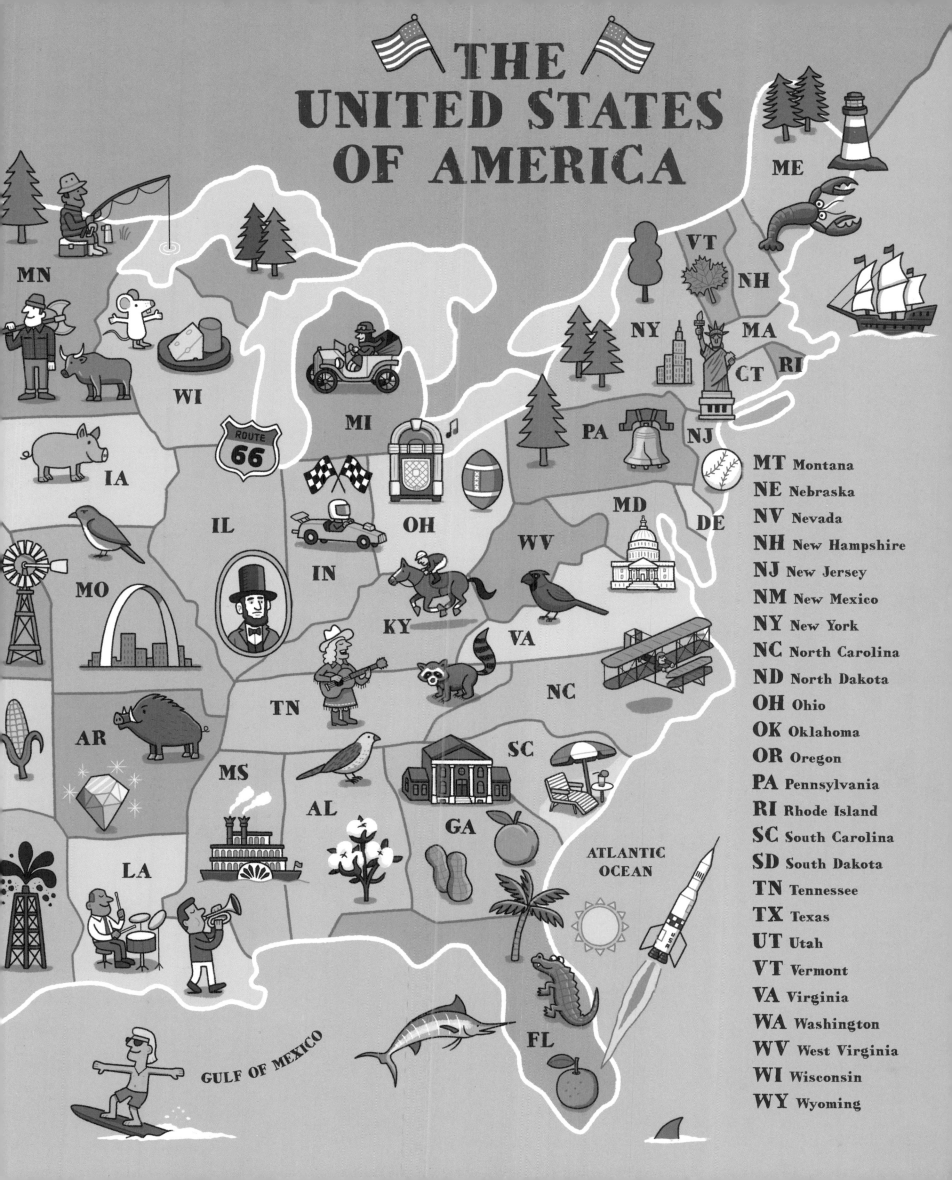

THE UNITED STATES OF AMERICA

ME

VT

NH

MA

CT RI

NY

PA

NJ

MN

WI

MI

OH

IL

IN

MD

DE

WV

MO

KY

VA

TN

NC

AR

MS

AL

SC

GA

LA

FL

ROUTE 66

ATLANTIC OCEAN

GULF OF MEXICO

MT Montana
NE Nebraska
NV Nevada
NH New Hampshire
NJ New Jersey
NM New Mexico
NY New York
NC North Carolina
ND North Dakota
OH Ohio
OK Oklahoma
OR Oregon
PA Pennsylvania
RI Rhode Island
SC South Carolina
SD South Dakota
TN Tennessee
TX Texas
UT Utah
VT Vermont
VA Virginia
WA Washington
WV West Virginia
WI Wisconsin
WY Wyoming

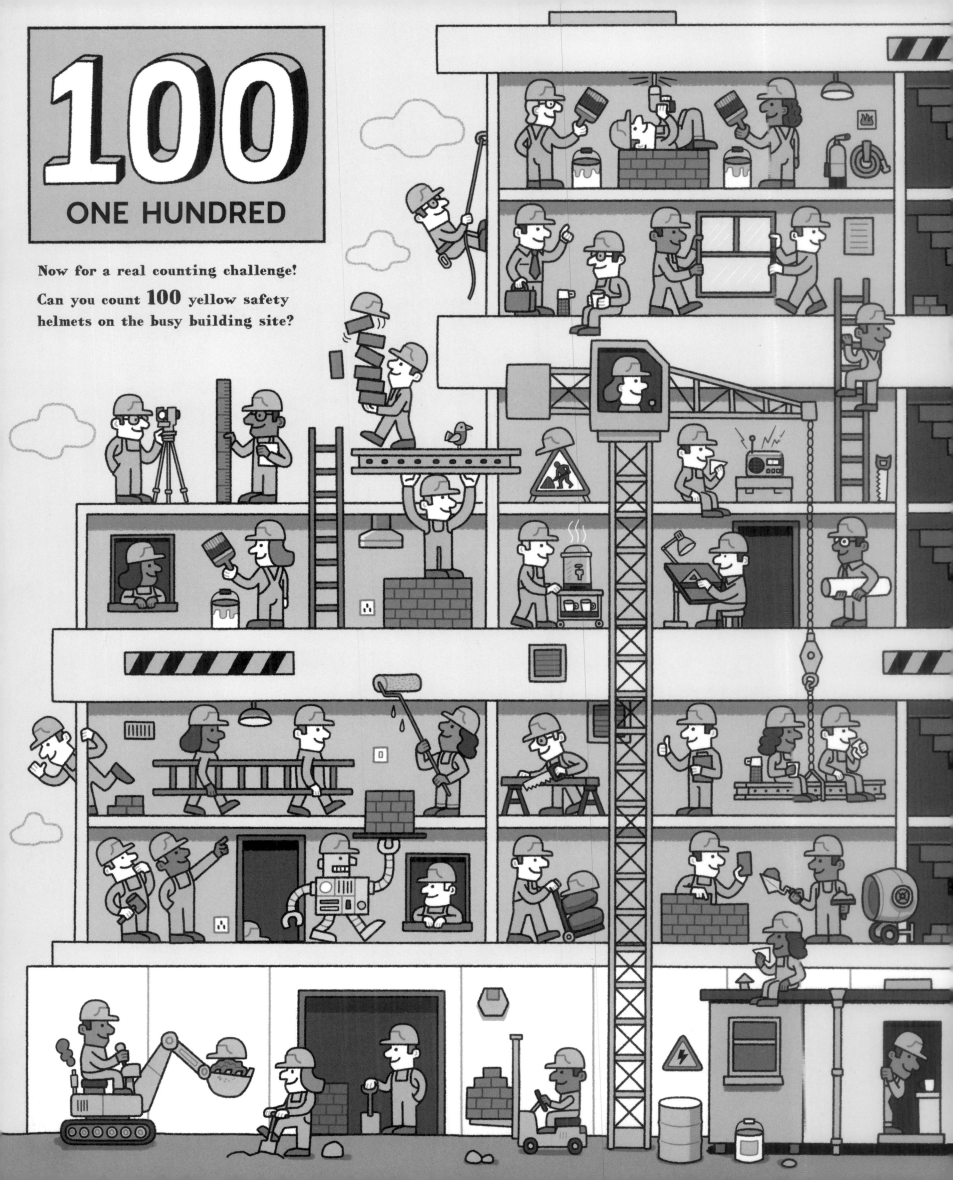

100
ONE HUNDRED

Now for a real counting challenge!
Can you count **100** yellow safety
helmets on the busy building site?